MADHUBALA

"I don't want to die…"

Compiled by
MANJU GUPTA

GENERAL PRESS

Published by
GENERAL PRESS
4805/24, Fourth Floor, Krishna House
Ansari Road, Daryaganj, New Delhi - 110002
Ph : 011-23282971, 45795759
E-mail : generalpressindia@gmail.com

www.generalpress.in

First Edition : 2018

ISBN : 9789387669253

Purchase our Books and eBooks online from:
Amazon.in | Flipkart.com | Infibeam.com

Published by Azeem Ahmad Khan for General Press

Printed at Repro Knowledgecast Limited, Thane

Contents

Madhubala *(Mumtaz Jehan Begum)* with her captivating smile

(1933 – 1969)

Preface

"*Allah, main marna nahin chahti...* (God, I don't want to die...)" was the plaintive cry of a bewitching beauty whose acting abilities in the Hindi cinema, be it a comedy, tragedy or romantic interlude, coupled with her tragic life story cut short by an incurable heart defect, established her as one of the most sought-after actresses in India. Her presence in public memory to this day becomes apparent when in a recent poll, she scored the maximum number of points for beauty and acting among all the actresses of Indian cinema – past and present. Her posters are still in demand and she is mentioned as one of the most beautiful faces of the Indian silver screen but whose "beauty attracted more attention than her talent." In 2004, nearly thirty-five years after her death, a digitally-coloured version of her film was released, in 2008

5

followed by a commemorative postage stamp, produced by India Post in a limited-edition presentation pack. The only other Indian actress to be so honoured was Nargis Dutt, who, not only a seasoned actress and a social worker too, passed away at a rather young age due to affliction with cancer.

Have you been able to identify about whom we are talking? It was none other than the beautiful and versatile actress of Hindi cinema – MADHUBALA, whose real life, marked by fame, wealth, drama, love, sorrow and heartbreak, ran hand in hand with the 'unrelenting diktat of destiny' till she breathed her last on 23 February 1969, shortly after her thirty-sixth birthday in that same month. The mere mention of her name conjures up an image of a stunning beauty with a mischievous, crooked smile and one who has left behind her memory in films for the posterity to relish her beauty and histrionics. As she led a very secluded life, partly due to her own liking but mostly in compliance with her father's wishes, very little is known about her except for what was written when she was alive and what has been narrated by those who had seen or known her from close quarters.

Madhubala's life cannot be viewed in isolation; mention must be made of her co-stars, directors, producers, singers, etc. with whom she interacted and whose contributions, apart from her own, went in to make some of her films all-time favourites. Hence, the period 1947 to 1960, when she was a formidable name in the Hindi film industry, was the golden age of Indian cinema – it was the era of film directors like Kedar Sharma, Mehboob Khan, Amiya Chakravorty, K.A. Abbas, Raj Kapoor, K. Asif and Bimal Roy; it was the period of musicians like Anil Biswas, Ghulam Haider, S.D. Burman, Sajjad Husain, Hemant Kumar, O.P. Nayyar, Khayyam, C. Ramchandra, Shankar-Jaikishen and Salil Choudhry; it was the time of magical voices like Shamshad Begum, Noor Jehan, Rajkumari, Amirbai Karnataki, Suraiya, Lata Mangeshkar, Mohammed Rafi, Mukesh, Talat Mehmood and Geeta Dutt; it was the season of poets like Sahir Ludhianvi, Shakeel Badayuni, Kaifi Azmi, Rajinder Kishen, Raja Mehdi, Majrooh Sultanpuri, Qamar Jalalabadi; and it saw the presence of a veritable galaxy of female heroines like Kamini Kaushal, Nalini Jayawant, Bina Rai, Nargis, Nimmi, and Nutan and their male counterparts like Dilip Kumar, Raj Kapoor, Dev Anand, Balraj Sahni, Motilal and others whose contributions are mentioned in glowing terms even today.

Childhood Years

When she was born as Mumtaz Jehan Begum Dehlavi in Delhi on 14 February 1933, St. Valentine's Day, a *najoomi* (fortune-teller), who was also known as *Kashmirwale Baba*, predicted that Mumtaz would have an astonishing future. The *najoomi* said, "*Badi hokar ye ladki bahot naam kamayegi, bahot paisa aur shohrat paayegi, lekin…*" (this girl will earn prestige, money and fame but…) and he paused and added that this girl would die before her age. All his predictions turned out to be true.

Born into an orthodox, middle-class Pathan family of Afghan origin, who could ever thought on seeing her that one day she would become famous as Madhubala, one of the most beautiful and versatile actresses of Hindi cinema? Her father Ataullah Khan was a dour and strict disciplinarian, who dominated both her life and career. He worked with the Imperial Tobacco Company in Peshawar, Pakistan, before coming to Delhi to start working as a driver for the same company. He did not stay here for long as, in the words of his youngest daughter Shahida, "My father worked with the Imperial Tobacco Company in Peshawar with the British. But being a Pathan, he was hot-headed and self-respecting. He couldn't bear being badly treated and lost a 15-year-old job in seconds."

Ataullah Khan's wife, Begum Ayeesha was a simple, illiterate woman who devoted her life to look after the home and the family. She gave birth to eleven children but three daughters and two sons died at the age of five and six. The six surviving daughters were Kaneez Fatima and Altaf before Mumtaz Jehan and three younger ones, named Chanchal, Zahida and Shahida. The last three addressed Mumtaz Jehan as 'Majhli Aapa', the second elder sister.

Ataullah Khan decided to relocate his family to Mumbai in the hope of making good, but the family had to endure unaccountable hardships. On 14 April 1944, a dock explosion and fire wiped away their small home, taking them to the streets. The family had a lucky escape as all of them had gone to see a film at a local theatre. Fortunately for them, a friend took them in, gave them shelter and food, and looked after them for seven months. Quite obviously this Pathan family had to undergo trying times as once Mumtaz Jehan herself recalled, "There were moments free of care and filled with joy. Then followed hardships and the heart-breaking effort to live and sustain oneself."

Shahida expressed her gratitude to her sister long after her death, "Right through my childhood, *Aapa* (as she addressed Mumtaz Jehan) remained busy shooting. Coming from a conservative Muslim family of Pathans, my father wasn't keen that we study. But fortunately, I was sent to St. Joseph's Convent, Bandra. Yes, she was the only earning member. She remained the earning member till the last. All that we are today, we owe it all to her."

Career as a Child Star

With his six remaining daughters to provide for, Ataullah Khan decided that his daughter Mumtaz Jehan, being the prettiest and brightest, would support them provided she could find a job in films. So, without a job for himself and with the young Mumtaz Jehan holding his hand, he began to frequent the film studios of Bombay in the hope of finding work. These film studios were in their backyard at Malad, where they would audition. It did not take long before Mumtaz Jehan bagged a role in Amiya Chakravorty's film '*Basant*' as Baby Mumtaz. In this film, which was released in 1942, she also sang two songs and one of them, *"Mere chhotey se man mein chhoti si duniya re…"* became immensely popular. At the tender age of nine, this marked her first step into the movie industry, which would provide financial sustenance to her family as long as she lived. A contemporary of Mumtaz Jehan was Nimmi, who, of the same age or so, saw this film and was captivated by Mumtaz Jehan's self-assured acting and song.

It seems Mumtaz Jehan took to acting as a fish takes to water and in one of her interviews, her sister Shahida said: "Our father brought all of us to Mumbai. *Aapa*, who was just seven, loved to sing and dance and was fond of music and poetry." In her very first film, *'Basant'*, Mumtaz Jehan sailed through like a veteran actor. Actor Ashok Kumar, who went on to act as her hero in many films, said that when he set eyes on her on the sets of one of his films at Bombay Talkies, he noticed Mumtaz Jehan pass the door of his make-up room and peep in nervously. When he asked her to come in, she ran away and, in his words, she 'never lost that innocence, that spark'.

Despite the success of this film, Ataullah Khan could not support his family and so took all the members back to Delhi to hunt for a job. In 1944, Amiya Chakravorty met the family again in Delhi to assign a role in his film *'Jwar Bhata'*, which she did not do but it prompted Ataullah Khan to settle down with his family at Malad, a suburb of Bombay, for good.

In 1944, Kedar Sharma of Ranjit Movietone made her act in his film, *'Mumtaz Mahal'*, wherein she impressed him with her talent. He said much later in life, "Acting seemed to be an instinct with her. There was lustre in her eyes, which expressed the great depths of her soul. Her diligence, discipline and ardour for work, for all of which Madhubala (Mumtaz Jehan) is so well known, were her notable qualities even as a child star. Her most important characteristic was her boundless eagerness to learn. Her devotion to duty, her desire to do her best and her dogged perseverance made me call her by the affectionate appel-lation, *ghaatan*."

Thespian Dilip Kumar, who was ten years older than her, remembers her as "a little girl who used to play around when I was in Bombay Talkies. She was plumpish, mischievous and very lively. But the aptitude and flair for acting were there from the beginning".

It was now time for Mumtaz to make a transition from child roles. So, after doing four more films – *'Dhanna Bhagat'* in 1945, *'Phoolwari', 'Pujari'* and *'Rajputani'* – all three in 1946, she acted as the heroine in Kedar Sharma's *'Neel Kamal'*.

Madhubala and Raj Kapoor as two newcomers in *'Neel Kamal'*

Successes and Failures

I n '*Neel Kamal*', 14-year old Mumtaz Jehan acted as a village belle opposite an atheist sculptor – the role assayed by Raj Kapoor, the 22-year old hero in his first film. Kedar Sharma said about his heroine, "Neither her looks, nor her raw talent impressed me as much as her intelligence and diligence. She worked like a machine, missed a meal, travelled daily in the overcrowded third-class compartments from Malad to Dadar and was never late or absent from work. Even at that age, the little lady knew her duty to her father, who had so many mouths to feed with no visible means of support." It was at this time that Ataullah Khan accepted other offers of films, but this annoyed Kedar Sharma, who considered her as "one of my products" and she, on her part, never stopped admitting, "Kedar Sharma was my 'guru' and I am proud to be his 'disciple'." But Ataullah Khan, as always, was "very stubborn. He hurt his own interests by this attitude. Here was too much discipline all around," said music director, Naushad.

This was also the time when she came to be compared with Marilyn Monroe and was rechristened Madhubala from Mumtaz Jehan by her close friend and mentor, Devika Rani, who admired her acting potential and good looks. The new name was found to fit her perfectly because she indeed was as a teenager, sweet as honey with her characteristic lopsided smile.

She acted with Raj Kapoor in three more films – '*Chittor Vijay*', '*Dil ki Rani*' and '*Amar Prem*', in which she was showered praise for her good looks. In 1948, her film '*Lal Dupatta*' won applause as she played the role of Shobha "beautifully and she proves herself at once competent and versatile in both light and pathetic sequences," said the magazine *Filmindia* of the 15-year old heroine. It continued, "'*Lal Dupatta*' is an attractive picture and the little Madhubala is its main attraction. This picture is the first milestone of her maturity in screen acting." She was even pitted against Suraiya, one of the topmost actresses of the time, in the film '*Singaar*' in 1949. It was said, "She (Madhubala) beats Suraiya hollow in every sequence they meet. Madhubala stores more emotions in a single face than would a thousand girls with as many faces"; when acting opposite Kamini Kaushal in '*Paras*' that very year, a critic wrote: "With her superb versatility, Madhubala makes Kamini Kaushal look like an amateur"; for '*Apradhi*', it was said, "The only silver lining to a long, dark cloud of boredom is the sparkling personality of Madhubala...In the heroine's role she beats everyone else hollow, though she has not much to beat and gives a versatile performance with sighs and smiles."

There were some films for which she was not spared either for her poor acting and these included '*Dulari*', for which she was indirectly criticised as she was "not nicely photographed as Dulari, the synthetic gypsy"; about the film '*Madhubala*', the magazine *Filmindia* commented, "The picture also proves that even a popular and talented star like Madhubala rushes to work in any picture without worrying about art, quality or even her own reputation as an artiste of talent." In this film she had acted out of a sense of gratitude for the help given by Ratibhai Seth when her sick mother had to be hospitalised. Even Dilip Kumar lamented, "Madhubala acted in more films than she should have." This could possibly be because she had to provide for her large family, as she was the only bread-earner.

Ten Best Songs Picturised on Madhubala

- *Jab pyar kiya to darna kiya...*
- *Ek pardesi mera dil le gaya...*
- *Achcha ji main haari, chalo maan jao na...*
- *Haal kaisa hai janaab ka...*
- *Aaiye meherbaan, baithiye jaan-e-jaan...*
- *Mera naam hai chin chin chu...*
- *Ayega, ayega, ayega anewala...*
- *Mohe panghat pe nandlal chhed gayo re...*
- *Ek ladki bheegi bhaagi si...*
- *Mohabbat ki jhooti kahani pe roye...*

From a Star to a Legend

Bombay Talkies, founded by Devika Rani and her first husband Himanshu Rai, gave Madhubala the next break after her first film *'Basant'* by producing *'Mahal'*, the third largest hit at the 1949 Indian box-office. Thus it was by 1950s, that Madhubala reached the pinnacle of glory plus success with this milestone film *'Mahal'*, directed by Kamal Amrohi and which ran to packed houses. It helped her carve a niche for herself in the annals of Indian film history. The story of the film was of unfulfilled love that is carried over from one life to the other and Madhubala "made a very beautiful spirit but, as an artist, she was very raw and required many retakes," said Ashok Kumar, the hero of the film. The key song *"Aayega aanewala..."* was used as a leitmotif for the spirit, to add to the mood of suspense and thrill and it helped to establish Lata Mangeshkar as the best playback singer in Indian cinema.

Madhubala as the haunting spirit in 'Mahal'

In 1950, Motilal acted in *'Hanste Ansu'* with the 17-year old Madhubala, who could not see her own movie as it had been classified as an adults' film, despite it not having anything objectionable. A critic noted, "It is not an easy job to steal a scene from these two (Motilal and Gope) seasoned artistes, but Madhubala did it."

In 1951, '*Tarana*' was released in which Madhubala and Dilip Kumar, both Devika Rani's discoveries, made a romantic team for the first time and triumphed together. She lost her heart to the hero in real life and about whom she told her sisters, "There's a luminous magnetism in his eyes like they have been filled with crushed pearls." This was a love which was to change her life and what a change it did! They became a romantic pair, appearing in a total of four films together, but this romance was jinxed and it was ordained to bring unhappiness and upheavals a galore in Madhubala's life. '*Tarana*' was followed by '*Sangdil*' and subsequently '*Amar*', which was a brilliant picture, but much ahead of its time. It did not do well at the box-office despite the presence of luminaries like Madhubala, Dilip Kumar and Nimmi.

In 1952, Madhubala acted opposite the tall, lanky and thin newcomer Shammi Kapoor in '*Jeevan Jyoti*', '*Rail ka Dibba*', '*Naqab*' and '*Boy Friend*'. He wanted to marry her but she had given her heart to Dilip Kumar by now. Shammi Kapoor said, "I had a very high regard and respect for her. Such people are just not made any longer and I am being very honest when I say this. Gita (Gita Bali, his wife) knew about it and my present wife also knows it. My life is an open book. I don't think I can ever forget her."

In the same period, Madhubala acted with Premnath in *'Badal'*, *'Aaraam'* and *'Saqi'*, and Premnath fell in love with her but had to give way when he discovered that she had eyes only for his friend, Dilip Kumar. Sister Shahida says, "*Aapa* first fell in love with Premnath. The relationship lasted six months. It broke on grounds of religion. He asked her to convert and she refused." Around this time, that is August 1952, Madhubala won interest in Hollywood too. She appeared in the American magazine, *Theatre Arts*, under the title, 'The Biggest Star in the World and She's not in Beverly Hills', describing her immense popularity in India. Academy-Award-winning director, Frank Capra, while attending the International Film Festival of India at Bombay, was keen to give her a break in Hollywood, but Madhubala's father, Ataullah Khan, declined the offer.

She gave a sterling comic performance as a spoilt heiress, Anita, in Guru Dutt's satire *'Mr. & Mrs. '55'*, released in 1955. During the shooting of this film, she would

often ask, 'How can I do this? What is this?' but as the
film progressed, she began to enjoy playing the part of
Mrs.'55. Film critic Bikram Singh said, "Any camera that
did not caress that face would be guilty of a crime."

Madhubala as the fiesty damsel with Guru Dutt in *'Mr. & Mrs. 55'*

In 1956, she acted in costume dramas such as '*Shirin-
Farhad*' and '*Raj-Hath*', and played a double role in the
social drama '*Kal Hamara Hai*' in 1959. In the mid-1950s,

her films, included some major ones, like Mehboob Khan's *'Amar'* (1954) which was based on the relationship between a lawyer, his educated fiancee and a village milkmaid. In a weak moment, the lawyer rapes the milkmaid despite being engaged to be married and goes into his shell due to his foolish act. This film did not do well commercially but those who appreciate good cinema would recall the scene where one sees a temple at the top of a lengthy flight of steps.

However, Madhubala bounced back between 1958 and 1960 when she starred in a series of hit films. These included *'Howrah Bridge'*, opposite Ashok Kumar where she played the role of an Anglo-Indian cabaret dancer and singer in Calcutta's Chinatown underworld. In the song *'Aaiye meherbaan...'* from this film, she lip-synched the song dubbed by Asha Bhosle and it remains popular to this day.

Among other successful films, she played opposite Bharat Bhushan in *'Phagun'*, in which O.P. Nayyar's music with songs like *'Ek pardesi mera dil le gaya...'* and *'Piya, piya na laage mora jeeya...'* created a stir; with Dev Anand in *'Kala Pani'* in which she was at her best in the song *'Achchaji main haari, chalo maan jao na...'* and

Raj Khosla, the director could not help but remark, "As a person she was warm, very gentle, very honest, very affectionate"; because at times she was amusing, then teasing, cajoling, hurt in an inimitable style of her own; in 1959, with her co-star Minu Mumtaz in '*Insaan Jaag Utha*', while passing through a most traumatic period of her life and which prompted the latter to offer her sympathy and advice without betraying her confidence; opposite Kishore Kumar in '*Chalti ka Naam Gaadi*'; and with Bharat Bhushan again in '*Barsaat ki Raat*' (1960).

The early 1960s also saw some of her intermittent releases like '*Jhumroo*' in 1961, '*Half Ticket*' in 1962 and '*Sharabi*' in 1964 but all of these performed above average at the box-office as they were marred by her absence and subsequent prolonged illness. On glancing at the Filmography at the end of this book, one finds that it was actually in the late '50s and early '60s that Madhubala gave hits one after another – '*Kala Pani*', '*Howrah Bridge*', '*Chalti ka Naam Gaadi*' and '*Barsaat ki Raat*' followed by the magnum opus, '*Mughal-e-Azam*'. Though a lot can be said about each of these films, but what journalist Jerry Pinto said comes immediately to one's mind, "Why is she still on everyone's list of wonderful Indian actresses? She was stunningly beautiful...she was a brilliant actress who could bring you to tears with '*Mohabbat ki jhooti kahani pe roye...*' Think of Madhubala and your memory turns into a kaleidoscope. Rain-drenched in '*Chalti ka Naam Gaadi*'; love-drenched as a feather teases her cheek in '*Mughal-e-Azam*'; the heiress who must marry to satisfy the conditions of her father's will in '*Mr. & Mrs. '55*'. There is a certain sensuousness that fills those memories. It is not just the appreciation of a lovely body; it isn't just that midriff in '*Mohe panghat pe Nandalal...*' It's the comfort with which she seemed to live in that body."

In '*Mughal-e-Azam*', Madhubala so well empathised with the character Anarkali that she and her role seemed to have merged into one. She reached the peak in histrionics in this film, which became her swan song.

For '*Bahut Din Huwe*', Madhubala went to Madras for shooting. After two days of work, she suddenly took very ill due to a hacking cough. In the morning, she brought up blood. Mr Vasan and his wife spent freely on her treatment and Madhubala later admitted, "He (Vasan) could easily have scrapped my brief spell of two days in the film and gone ahead without me, but he said, 'For your sake, I'll abandon the picture if necessary.' I will never forget the kindness I received from Mr S.S. Vasan and his wife."

Madhubala acted in as many as 66 films from 1947 to 1964, but only 15 of these proved box-office successes, despite her stupendous acting abilities. Dilip Kumar regrets, "Had she lived, and had she selected her films with more care, she would have been far superior to her contemporaries…"

In his autobiography, Dilip Kumar reveals that K. Asif was trying to make capital of Dilip and Madhubala's emotional involvement when filming the classic scene in *Mughal-e-Azam* where the feather comes between their lips and which had set the imagination of many on fire. He says that the scene was shot "when we had completely stopped even greeting each other. It should in all fairness, go down in the annals of film history as a tribute to the artistry of two professionally committed actors, who kept aside personal differences and fulfilled the directorial vision of a sensitive, arresting and sensuous screen moment to perfection."

Ethereal Beauty

Her exceptionally good looks made her the talk of the film industry. Baburao Patel of *Filmindia* described her as being "gifted with a rare beauty and captivating grace." He would often say that she was "easily our most talented, most versatile and best-looking artiste." Director O.P. Dutta said, "Her smile was a veritable celebration of living." Film actress Nadira proclaimed, "She was ecstatically, exasperatingly beautiful," while her contemporary Nimmi, on seeing her during the shooting of '*Amar*', passed sleepless nights thinking how she would fare against "this apparition, this angel in human shape".

Producer-director Manmohan Desai remarked, "She was the only true beauty to grace the Indian screen and she was beautiful in every film with no exceptions."

Gifted with a rare beauty

Filmfare, the film magazine said, "Her complexion is moon-kissed and the smile – an irresistible come-hither but stay-where-you-are smile." Photographer J.H. Thakker said, "She was a cameraman's delight." Recollects Minu

Mumtaz, "Her complexion was so fair and translucent that when she ate a *paan* (betel leaf), you could almost see the red colour going down her throat." Dilip Kumar told *Filmfare* in 1990, "Madhubala's beauty was so overpowering that in paying homage to it, people have missed out on a lot of her other attributes. Of course, she was beautiful, though I don't think hers was a perfectly chiselled face. She had a slightly accentuated nose, though it didn't take away from the totality of her beauty. Yes, she was beautiful in totality."

An interesting incident is narrated about her delicate skin. Madhubala was prone to getting pimples due to strong studio lights and heavy cosmetics. She therefore did not attend one day's shooting but devoted one extra day to make up for the loss caused to the producer. It is also said that she suffered from irrational fears and anxieties. These included using water for drinking and bathing only from a certain Parsi well near Flora Fountain. Her co-star Minu Mumtaz justified this by saying that Madhubala's skin was so delicate that if "pressed hard, a blue patch would appear" and that she was allergic to any other water.

An episode is narrated regarding her film 'Raj Hath' a few days after its opening night when she stole into the cinema hall in a *burqa* and accompanied by her sister and a friend. This friend had to say that Madhubala wore a printed pink *kurta,* black *shalwar* and black *dupatta,* apart from earrings and red lipstick. Her friend admitted, "I have never seen anyone look lovelier. I could not stop gazing at her." It was with this friend that sometimes Madhubala went out for shopping to Dadar for cotton saris.

Incidentally when B.K. Karanjia first laid his eyes on Madhubala in person, he wrote, "I was quite stunned. I wasn't prepared for the woman I saw. It was as if a vision of beauty had achieved form and presence right in front of my eyes…she was probably the most beautiful girl I'd ever seen in my life. Dark brown eyes, reddish brown hair, height about five feet six inches, fair with the peaches and cream complexion of English girls, totally without make-up and dressed simply in a white sari. A very, very desirable woman!"

Her sister Shahida admits, "What do I say of her beauty? The fact that she's spoken about even 42 years after she passed away is proof enough. We suffered from a complex when we stood beside her. Being Pathans, we were all tall, fair and had long hair, but none of us sisters looked like her. Our mother was short. We had taken after our father. But we weren't a patch on *Aapa*."

A strange chemistry at work between Madhubala and her beau Dilip Kumar

Madhubala herself admitted once, "To be beautiful means a lot to me, but not everything. Happiness comes first."

In his autobiography *Dilip Kumar: The Substance and the Shadow,* Dilip Kumar admits, "I was attached to her both as a fine co-star and as a person who had some of the attributers I hoped to find in a woman of that age and time. We had viewers admiring our pairing in *'Tarana'* and our working relationship was warm and cordial. She, as I said earlier, was very sprightly and vivacious and, as such, she could draw me out of my shyness and reticence effortlessly. She filled a void that was crying out to be filled – not by an intellectually sharp woman but a spirited woman whose liveliness and charm were the ideal panacea for the wound that was taking its own time to heal."

As a Person

Madhubala was not only ravishingly beautiful and a versatile actress, at home in both emotional and comical roles, she was very simple in her appearance in real life. She preferred a natural look, unadorned by heavy make-up or bright clothes and jewellery. The eyes worked their own magic, the skin had its own glow and her brown tresses left unfettered would blow carelessly across her face. Unalloyed and pure, her beauty belongs to every age.

A memorable incident is narrated about Madhubala when she was in her teens. It so happened that her pregnant mother fell seriously ill and as her condition worsened,

No make-up or jewellery adorned her beautiful face

Madhubala approached Ratibhai Seth, nephew of Chandulal Shah for help. Ratibhai immediately gave her 3,000 rupees. At that time she was earning a meagre 300 rupees a month. It was then that she decided that whenever anyone would be in need and approach her for help, she would never refuse.

Madhubala was very punctual at the studios and more often than not, she was at the studios before her director or hero. *Filmindia* went to the extent of saying, "With the time-conscious Madhubala reaching the studios at 9 a.m. sharp, Mehboob has to pass through the pain of going early with all his technicians. They all come yawning and wake up Dilip Kumar who sleeps in the studio these days to be in time for his heroine."

On the first day of shooting for Sohrab Modi's film '*Raj Hath*', she reached the studios at the prescribed time of 8.30 a.m. The gate and the make-up room were still closed and no one was around. The next morning, everyone was ready for work and the embarrassed Sohrab Modi himself was present, when her car drove in.

For the making of Dev Anand's production, '*Kala Pani*', she was ready with make-up when he drove into the studio. She made no comment, merely saying with a laugh, "*Assalaam alaikum producer saheb*." Co-star Nadira corroborated this by saying, "I was in the studio that day. She was coming out of the make-up room and his car was coming inside. '*Assalaam alaikum producer saheb*' – she said it so sarcastically with a laugh, as much as to say, you being the producer are coming now, while I am ready with make-up on. In other words, you should have been here much before me." Later, even Dev Anand admitted, "When Madhubala is on the sets, one often goes much ahead in the schedule."

Shahida reveals, "She even went to watch movies in a *burqa*. *Aapa* became a craze because she was never seen in public. She wasn't allowed to attend any function, any premiere. She had no friends. But she never resisted; she was obedient. Being protective, my father earned the reputation of being domineering. He was asked why he'd made her join films in the first place. He'd say, 'I had 12 children. We would've starved to death. I've lost my sons, who could've been my support'. *Aapa* was emotional by nature. She'd be in tears in seconds. We'd keep wondering what had happened and she'd laugh easily too. The moment she began laughing, she couldn't stop. So that day's shooting had to be cancelled! She wasn't religious, but was God-fearing. She didn't fast but prayed once a day."

Equally expressive when laughing or pensive

Regarding her simplicity, her sister said, "She loved wearing plain white saris. At home she'd wear maxis. She loved *mogras* in her hair. She was fond of gold and *kundan* jewellery. She was also fond of *sher-o-shayari* as she knew a bit of Urdu. An English tutor also came home to teach her. She loved eating *chaat, ragda patties, pani puri* and *kulfi*. She'd never diet. Those days actresses were healthy women, not size zero! She'd drive all of us to Chowpatty in her imported cars, Hillman, Buick and Station Wagon, but she'd wear a *burqa* to hide her identity. When she'd be pulled up by the traffic police for that, she'd plead, 'Please let me wear it or else I'll get mobbed'."

On account of her characteristic aloofness and the aura of mystery surrounding her because of her reclusive life, the aura of a 'star' engulfed her and vast crowds would wait at the gates of the studios, just to catch a glimpse of her.

When asked about her inherent dislike for publicity and adoption of seclusion, Madhubala had once admitted that she did not wish to "attend the kind of functions where only the current favourites are invited and where a decade or two hence, I will not be invited."

In the studios it was discussed that she did not eat food or even water from anywhere else but from her home because she always carried her own food and water. She seemed to be rather finicky and it is said that though she went out of her way to avoid any unbecoming situation to develop, she seemed to have rubbed her producer,

P.L. Santoshi the wrong way when he was shooting 'Nirala'. He asked her to wade through deep waters in a stream at Ghodbunder but Madhubala refused. She wanted water to be brought from her home with which she could wash herself later, possibly because she suffered from some irrational fears and anxieties. P.L. Santoshi did not take kindly to his heroine's behaviour and ordered a 'pack-up' and even stayed away from work for four days. He narrated this incident to B.K. Karanjia who promptly published the story under the title 'Blundering in Wonderland', in his magazine, *Movie Times*. He wrote the entire episode and added, "On the fourth day, as Santoshi was going home, his car passed Madhubala's, with Khan Saheb in it. Khan Saheb asked his driver to overtake Santoshi's car, which done, he got out and stopped Santoshi, standing in the middle of the road with outstretched hands. He told the director that Madhu was terribly upset and had stopped eating. She wanted to apologise to him and would deem it a favour if he visited her. Santoshi obliged. She apologised and shooting resumed the next day."

This matter was resolved amicably but it led to a confrontation of unforeseeable dimensions because the press, which had already been smarting with anger on being refused permission to visit her shooting sessions, ganged up to criticise her; some even went to the extent of threatening to disfigure her. This really frightened the daughter and father. Baburao Patel of *Filmindia* was the only journalist to desist from attacking her. It was only when the ban was lifted on the journalists that the war was called off and Karanjia wrote: "The next Sunday the journalists were invited to Madhubala's residence – 'Arabian Villa' – for tea. The 'war' was well and truly over at last. At the villa's gate, along with the security guards, stood Khan Saheb, with a genial smile, welcoming us journalists, eight or nine of us."

Karanjia even wrote later about her, saying she had "a slightly naughty side to her personality and a wonderful sense of humour. She was always playing pranks on people. Sometimes, it took a serious turn because they began to imagine she was in love with them; she was only joking." Even a number of other people have said that she indulged in playful flirtation.

"Before she was even 20 years old, she had got everything – money, bungalows, cars, clothes and jewellery; the last named she hardly wore. As for clothes, she did have some dazzling clothes, but these were pushed at the back of the cupboard and one hardly ever saw her in these. In any case she hardly went out, except to go for drives in her car as she loved driving." She even confessed once, "I am not a spendthrift for the simple reason that I don't know what to spend money on. I do not have a passion for jewellery or clothes. I do not travel; I do not go out much. By God's grace, I have all the necessities of life and I am happy."

With few and far between opportunities to strike close friendships due to the strict upbringing of her father, her only exposure was to a few colleagues in the studio. She was not seen at parties, premieres, picnics, races, fund-raising drives, cricket matches or film festivals which other stars frequented to gain popularity. Even location shooting was limited to spots close to Bombay. A glittering function was to be held for the release of her film, 'Amar', when a journalist asked her if she would make an exception and be present for the occasion. She replied, "I'd be scared to death. Once I have finished at the studio, I do not want to be Madhubala, the star."

Despite all the restrictions imposed on her, her natural effervescence and ready laughter could not be curbed, especially with those with whom she had struck a friendly rapport and to whom she could reveal her secrets.

Another characteristic about her which one seldom sees in other female stars is that the green-eyed monster of jealousy never troubled her and she was fulsome in her praise of some of the other stars. About Gita Bali, she said, "A sheer delight to watch" and of Meena Kumari, "She has a unique voice. No other heroine has it."

Shahida says, "*Aapa* was emotional by nature. She'd be in tears in seconds. We'd keep wondering what had happened and she'd laugh easily too. The moment she began laughing, she couldn't stop."

At times, it was these fits of laughter that landed her in trouble with her co-stars. Once during the shooting of '*Amar*', while Nimmi was dancing before Dilip Kumar, she missed her step and Madhubala burst into her characteristic giggles. This, as expected, hurt Nimmi, but Madhubala later realised her mistake and apologised to Nimmi.

On the sets of '*Mughal-e-Azam*', Madhubala again burst into laughter when her co-star Nigar Sultana was giving a scene. This time her laughter turned into tears when Nigar Sultana lambasted her for her behaviour.

It is said, that this event had hurt Nigar Sultana so much that even after more than 40 years and with Madhubala having left for her heavenly abode, Nigar Sultana mentioned the incident in an unforgiving tone.

It is said that Madhubala did the film *'Madhubala'* for Movietone simply for the reason that she felt a sense of gratitude for the financial help that Ratibhai Seth had given her when her sick mother needed to be hospitalised. She had not forgotten this and thus went out of her way to accommodate the banner. She said later, "It meant turning down a couple of starring roles, even returning the advance paid to me by one of them. It was my turn to stretch out a helping hand and I did so with my work in a film to which I even gave my name Madhubala."

What is little known is that she made huge donations for charitable causes. In the year 1950, there was an inflow of East Bengali refugees from East Pakistan (now Bangladesh) and so moved was she at their plight that she donated Rs 50,000, which was a huge amount at that period of time. She personally handed over the cheque and letter to Home Minister of Bombay, Morarji Desai, saying, "It is not fair I think of those who are fortunate enough to enjoy the best blessings of God to sit and watch with indifference the sufferings of others..." Morarji Desai not only thanked her but showed his appreciation for her father to allow her to make such a fat contribution.

She used to treat the studio workers every now and then with sweets and if anyone asked her for money, she never refused. There was a man who had once brought a message for her from Dilip Kumar and subsequently he made it a practice to borrow money from her on some pretext or other. When she was told that he was exploiting her kind nature, she admitted candidly, "Yes, I know he is cheating me, but how can I refuse him? Let him have what he wants. He brings in Yusuf's (Dilip Kumar) name." So strong were her feelings for Dilip Kumar that everything was pardoned.

One day when Dilip Kumar's younger brother Ehsan Khan dropped in at the studio and he saw a new car parked outside, he asked her if it was her car. She immediately handed him the keys, saying, "Go and take a drive."

Life, a Struggle

F ame brought no major changes in her life as she continued to lead a cloistered existence at home. As she had started working at a very young age, she did not attend school, but was proficient in Urdu and Pashtu. She did not know English but Sushila Rani Patel, wife of Baburao Patel who brought out the film magazine, *Filmindia*, began tutoring her in the language. Being a bright pupil, Madhubala learnt to speak, read and write the language in no time.

In the film industry, she was considered as "one of the most well-behaved girls," said Anil Biswas, film director. At the studios, she showed "no *nakhraas*, no fuss and never let her work suffer…Madhu was very unworldly and credulous and was always afraid of being mobbed," added her friend Salma Irani, an assistant director.

At home and within the family, the atmosphere was very restrictive. Madhubala's day began at six in the morning when she would be the first person to reach the studio. Says her youngest sister, Shahida, "*Abba* (father) was a disciplinarian. *Aapa* had to begin shooting at 9 a.m. At 6 p.m., the car would be sent to the studio and she'd be brought home. My father never went to the studio." Night shootings were not allowed, except in the case of her film '*Mughal-e-Azam*'. Even outdoor shootings were not permitted and nor did she attend film functions, thus being kept at arm's length from the glitter and shine of the bright world. Visitors to the house were not encouraged and as a result, Madhubala tended to meet strangers with wariness and caution before her ready laughter took over. Once she had established a rapport, she would confide all about herself to the new friend, which included Gulshan Ewing, editor of *Filmfare*, actresses Nimmi, Kammo, Minu Mumtaz, Nadira and B.K. Karanjia, who was the editor of *Movie Times* magazine. Sister Shahida says, "*Abba* was protective and inculcated discipline, but that doesn't mean he was harsh and difficult. My sister was very beautiful and he wanted to ensure no harm came her way. He did not allow her to attend parties because he was aware that men who drank could misbehave."

Co-star Nimmi said about her, "She never went anywhere apart from the studios. No one could come on her sets, no guests, no journalists. She went to no one's house, no one came to hers. She attended no filmland functions. This kept her so remote that it was not just the public, even we, in the film industry, were in awe of her. Her father's restrictions had created a certain aura around her."

Possibly this restricted life made film journalist Ram Aurangabadkar complain once, "She lacked warmth; *bahut rookhi si thi"* (very detached and dry she was). But B.K. Karanjia countered this by saying that she was regal in her behaviour with nothing cheap or vulgar about her. "There was something startlingly different about her from the other stars, as if she carried an aura about her."

So she lived like an obedient daughter, giving in to the dictates of her father who decided with whom she acted, which films she signed, what she was paid and how her money was invested – be it invested in failed ventures like films titled, 'Pathan', 'Sayyad', 'Shan-e-Awadh', 'Mehbooba' and 'Lali Chandan'. Even co-star Dilip Kumar remarked on this later, "Unfortunately a good lot of the revenue she had earned was dissipated in futile attempts at picture making."

The magazine *Filmfare* said, "The great success and adulation of fans had not spoilt Madhubala. Her pleasures centred around the members of her family, a simple household presided over by the dour but loving father, who dictates the home policy to the complete satisfaction of all concerned." She herself reminisced rather fondly on looking back on her childhood, "The gentle caring eyes of my mother and the hearty laughter of my beloved father as with his finger held firmly in my hand, I walked with him." Thus, while acknowledging the immense effort required to sustain herself and her family, she admitted, "Never for one moment, and I speak with complete honesty, was I left loveless and lonely."

Strange as it may seem to those who had seen Ataullah Khan exercising control over all her activities to believe what sister Shahida has to say about her father, "He was not difficult as is believed. He was disciplined and insisted on punctuality. That was what she imbibed too. Once she was to shoot at Ranjit Studio, but there were heavy rains. *Abba* said, 'You must go; your name shouldn't be tarnished.' Those days Ranjit Studio was a 15-minute drive from our home in Bandra, though it took her an hour-and-a-half to reach. The gates were locked. No one had turned up. She waited for half an hour and returned."

Madhubala preferred a veil of secrecy around her

In the book titled *Self-Portrait,* published in 1962, the authors Harish Booch and Karing Doyle say, "Unlike other stars, Madhubala prefers a veiled secrecy around her and is seldom seen in social gatherings or public functions" and contrary to popular belief "Madhubala is rather simple and unassuming." This is echoed in Shahida's interview to *Filmfare:* "(Madhubala) became a craze because she was never seen in public. She wasn't allowed to attend any function, any premiere. She had no friends. But she never resisted; she was obedient. Being protective, my father earned the reputation of being domineering."

Regarding her popularity, Dilip Kumar said, "She was extremely popular…and I think the only star for whom people thronged outside the gates. Very often, when shooting was over, there'd be a vast crowd standing at the gates just to have a look at Madhu…it wasn't so for anyone else. That was her personal effect on her fans. Her personality was vivacious."

Given the nature of her beliefs and her inherently emotional temperament, it was really no surprise at all that when Madhubala fell in love, she committed herself totally and for life. "Madhu loved only one man," confirmed her sister Kaneez Fatima, "and that was Dilip Kumar, till the day she died."

Madhubala had once admitted, "I am very emotional. I have always lived my life with my heart. For that I have suffered more than is necessary. I have been hurt."

Unfulfilled Love

Though Madhubala is accused of falling in love with Kamal Amrohi, Premnath, Pradeep Kumar and Bharat Bhushan, the real love of her life was the thespian Dilip Kumar. At the age of eleven she had met Dilip Kumar on the sets of *'Jwar Bhata'* but it was at 18 that Cupid struck when she met him on the sets of *'Tarana'*, in 1951. It is said that while the shooting was going on, she sent her female hairdresser with a note written in Urdu along with a red rose, asking him to accept it if he loved her. This, as expected, amused him and which he did accept later on. They became a romantic pair, appearing in a total of four films together.

Surprisingly, though Madhubala was not seen at any event, on two occasions she was seen outside the studios or home. She attended the premieres of 'Bahut Din Huwe' in 1954 and 'Insaniyat' in 1955, as both the films were produced by S.S. Vasan's Gemini Studios. The first film did not win any applause for her and in the second, she had not even acted, but because the Vasans had taken great care of her when she fell seriously ill in Madras during the shooting of 'Bahut Din Huwe', she could not ignore their kindness. The premiere of 'Insaniyat' was significant as it was the first time that she was escorted by Dilip Kumar. Journalist Pandit K. Razdan wrote in his autobiography, "The sight of Madhubala and Dilip Kumar entering the Roxy Cinema holding hands can never fade out from the screen of my memory." This occasion was captured by cameras as journalists went into a tizzy, capturing the image of Madhubala in love. She never looked more happier than that day. The early fifties were Madhubala's best years. She was rapturously and ecstatically in love and exuded happiness.

Recalling those days, Gulshan Ewing wrote: "For a while, she thrust on me the mantle of 'confidante'. Many were the whispered conversations she had with me, all rustling with the same rhythm – Yusuf, Yusuf, Yusuf. She was so in love that light leapt out and dazzled everyone. She would squeal when his name was mentioned; she would blush and perspire when his presence was imminent."

Dilip Kumar and Madhubala were both very private persons and their meetings were away from the public eye. "They went out for drives after shooting," said a friend, "or she picked him up on her way to the studios. She'd sound the horn and he came out and joined her. She did not enter his house. It looked very much like they'd get married any day."

Madhubala's affair lasted nine years with Dilip Kumar. Why did it end? Why did it not materialise into the bond of marriage, when both were from the same field, same Pathan families and equally devoted to each other?

During the making of '*Dhake ki Malmal*' in 1956, and in the presence of actor Om Prakash, events of a dramatic nature took place that decided the final shape of the association between Dilip and Madhubala. Om Prakash was on the sets of the film when he was startled by a message from Dilip Kumar, who asked to see him.

Dilip was with Madhubala in her make-up room and the atmosphere was surcharged. Om Prakash was requested to simply sit down and be a witness to the happenings. He watched as Dilip Kumar implored Madhubala, asking her to go with him and be married that very day. He had a *qazi* ready and waiting at his home and he wanted her to leave with him immediately. "I will marry her today," he emphasised. Apparently some source had said Madhubala and Dilip had got secretly engaged.

"It was the condition that he put forth that became the stumbling block – she would have to leave her father and never meet him again. Madhubala's refrain was that this was impossible, and apart from this, she said nothing. Dilip Kumar urged her repeatedly, again and again. He asked if this meant she was not willing to marry him? He told her if he went away now, he would never return. Madhubala was silent. At last, he got up and left – alone and out of her life," said Om Prakash. Their stormy relationship lasted about nine years.

It has been said that the veracity of Dilip Kumar's condition to marry Madhubala, provided she broke off all ties with her family, is questionable. It would be safe to say that he may have felt a deep resentment towards Ataullah Khan because it was only on the actual film set, or in the movie studio that the couple was allowed to interact, and that too only behind the back of the elder Khan. Their rendezvous had to be kept hidden. For Madhubala to be under the watchful eye of her father had always been her whole way of life, but for Dilip Kumar, it must have felt like a huge imposition.

It is surmised that Ataullah Khan did not approve of this affair because his whole family was dependent on Madhubala and it never occurred to him that she was entitled to a life of her own at some stage. Despite the deep love that she harboured for Dilip Kumar, she could not muster the courage to defy her father. She was caught between Scylla and Charybdis so to say – Dilip Kumar's love on one side and Ataullah's acceptance on another. Her loyalty pulled her in opposing directions and she could not make up her mind.

A crisis occurred in her life when she signed for B.R. Chopra's film 'Naya Daur', co-starring Dilip Kumar.

Ten days of indoor shooting was over when a long stint of outdoor shooting near Bhopal was announced. Madhubala's father Ataullah Khan refused to send her on location shooting. This led to a deterioration of events as Ataullah Khan had already taken an advance payment of Rs 30,000 which he refused to return. Chopra terminated her role and this riled her father. Location shooting would have meant long periods of absence and allowing Dilip Kumar to spend time with Madhubala without any restrictions. Ataullah Khan said that he had made it clear to every producer that his daughter's heart disease did not allow her to travel to distant locations, miles away from any doctor. Chopra took the father-and-daughter duo to court where allegations and counter-allegations flowed. Dilip Kumar, who was deeply in love with Madhubala, gave strong evidence against her to prompt R.D. Chadha, a junior advocate in the case, to say, "He was so inimical in his attitude towards her at the trial that she turned round to me in court on one occasion and said, 'I wonder if this is the same man who loved me and whom I loved'!" Actually the anger that Dilip Kumar harboured at her father's refusal to allow the marriage to take place prodded the former to be so adamant and not forgive. Chadha later said, "I tried my best to tell Dilip Kumar, whatever it be, don't go to court. But he only replied, 'I am trapped'." Madhubala gauged the demise of her love affair. She was hurt deeply and out of shock and distress, she cried in the court.

Madhubala's sisters mentioned that their sister died twice, first when the split between her and Dilip Kumar was confirmed. Her youngest sister Shahida said, "*Aapa* met *Bhaijan* (Dilip Kumar) on the sets of '*Tarana*'. They later worked in '*Sangdil*', '*Amar*' and '*Mughal-e-Azam*'. It was a nine-year long affair. They even got engaged. *Unki Aapa ayi thi, chunni lekar* (his sister had come with a *chunni* as is the custom). *Bhaijan* was also a Pathan." But Ataullah Khan refused to give them permission to marry.

Dilip Kumar said, "She was a very, very obedient daughter," who in spite of her success, fame and wealth, submitted to the domination of her father and more often than not, paid for his mistakes. But Shahida counters this allegation by saying, "Contrary to reports, my father never stopped her from getting married. We already had enough money by then and were financially secure. *Aapa* and *Bhaijan* looked made for each other. He'd often come home. He has even seen me in my school uniform.

He was respectful towards us and addressed us with '*aap*'.
The two would go for a drive or sit in the room and talk."

Then in 1960, she appeared in the magnum opus
'*Mughal-e-Azam*', which marked one of her greatest
performance as the doomed courtesan *Anarkali*. She gave
an outstanding performance in an outstanding movie –
her last. During the making of this film, Dilip Kumar
was in the habit of dropping by to see Madhubala even
when he was not required for the day's shooting. He came
on her sets and, if she was working, nothing was said.
He stood watching; wordless glances were exchanged
and he left, but his very presence was enough to trans-
port Madhubala into a world of happiness. She looked
forward to these few moments with all her heart, her eyes
searching for him. When she saw him, her day was made.

The immensity of her affection seemed to permeate
her whole being with a glow and radiance, prompting
Filmindia to comment: "Madhubala has found her soul
at last in the company of Dilip Kumar." Her moorings
still intact, life moved on an even keel. Meetings with Dilip
Kumar took place discreetly, well away from the public
eye, at times in the homes of friends like Sushila Rani
Patel, or K. Asif and his wife Sitara Devi. According to

Sitara Devi: "They used to come over often. Asif and I used to go out so that they could have some privacy."

Shammi Kapoor remembers that when they were shooting for '*Naqab*' at the Prabhat Studios in Poona, Dilip Kumar would drive down from Bombay to meet Madhubala. He even flew to Bombay to spend Eid with her, taking time off from his shooting stint for Gemini's '*Insaniyat*' in Madras. The romance was all too apparent on the screen, where it was reaffirmed in Madhubala's expressive eyes and smiles, and in Dilip Kumar's equally eloquent intensity. If the romantic scenes of '*Mughal-e-Azam*' stand out as a class apart and continue to weave their spell on viewers even today, it is largely due to that spark of truth which runs through them, manifesting itself in a palpable under-current of passion. The same could be said of '*Tarana*', '*Amar*', of '*Sangdil*' in varying degrees.

Shahida insists, "The breakup with Dilip Kumar happened due to the court case during '*Naya Daur*' in the mid '50s. The unit was to shoot somewhere in Gwalior. During the shooting of another film with Jabeen Jaleel, at the same location, a mob had attacked the women and even torn their clothes off. My father was wary and just asked that the locale be changed. It's not that he didn't

A sterling performance by Madhubala in 'Mughal-e-Azam'

let her go outdoors. *Aapa* had shot in Mahableshwar, Hyderabad and other places before. *Bhaijan* called my father 'a dictator' in court and sided with the Chopras (late B.R. Chopra was the director). *Dararein pad gayee, rishtey toot gaye* (relationships were broken). We love and respect *Bhaijan* but I have just one question, '*Aapki mohabbat yahi thi, aapki chahat yahi thi, phir aapne aisa kyun kiya* (why didn't you side with your love)?' *Bhaijan* could have simply said let's change the location or else remained neutral. *Aapa* used to cry a lot those days. They had conversations on the phone, trying to patch up. He kept saying, 'Leave your father and I'll marry you'. She'd say, 'I'll marry you but just come home, say sorry and hug him'. It was *zid* (stubborn attitude) which destroyed their love. But my father never asked her to break the engagement or ever demanded an apology from him."

Shahida continued, "Yes, a lot was printed about how she was very 'romantic' and had many affairs. Let me make this clear, I swear to God that this is not true. Of course, the industry is a man's world and as co-actors, she indulged in a bit of friendly banter with men, but everything got converted to linkages. 'Flirting' was the word used at that time. In that era, there were also gentlemen like Premnathji, who was linked to her after they co-starred in '*Baadal*' and '*Saaqi*'. Premnathji actually came and proposed to her, saying 'Madhu, I want to marry you.' But she declined, saying our father was very strict and wouldn't approve of it. Just let me make it clear that she had once fallen in love with Dilip Kumar and married

Kishore Kumar, Madhubala was confined to her bed in the last days of her life. She repeatedly watched her favourite movies, '*Mughal-e-Azam*', '*Barsaat ki Raat*', '*Chalti ka Naam Gaadi*' and '*Mahal*'. She used to recite Urdu poems to herself and saw the song from '*Mughal-e-Azam*' – '*Pyar kiya to darna kya…*' over 500 times."

Among the very few reflections made by Madhubala, one of them was a chilling evidence of the disastrous consequences of the break-up on her mind and heart. All the underlying bitterness, the sense of betrayal and dejection come through as she spoke of "the innumerable sorrows and few joys that life had given her." She had said, "The sum total of my life is a bitter experience which is coiled tight like a spring within my heart and when released, hurts excruciatingly. It is true that one learns something from every experience but when the experience is evil, the shock is so great that one feels as though one can never recover from it."

Shahida asserts that her sister nearly died when the '*Naya Daur*' disaster cemented the split and stilled the bubbling laughter, "During the court case, Dilip Kumar supported B.R. Chopra and that hurt my sister. They were supposed to get married; instead, a wonderful couple broke up." This gave Ataullah Khan the opportunity to taunt his daughter, "You claim he loves you. Is this love?"

Journalist Bunny Reuben was asked to write an article on her for *Filmfare*. He visited her home and she looked very excited to meet him, possibly because she knew that he was close to Dilip Kumar. Reuben said, "She wanted to talk only about her Yusuf Khan (Dilip Kumar); doing the feature was secondary. As she proceeded to unburden herself of all the intimate and hurtful details of their relationship, she put her head on my shoulder and wept uncontrollably...She wanted me to go and convince him how badly he had treated her and how much she still loved him." Moved by her plight, Reuben found a suitable opportunity to talk to Dilip Kumar and said, "She still carries a torch for you, Yusuf". He shot back, "What bloody torch?" At this outburst, Reuben did not have the courage to dish out the details of his meeting with Madhubala.

This fatal blow to the Dilip-Madhubala relationship made Dilip Kumar say that he felt 'trapped' and friend Shammi Kapoor went on to say, "This inability to leave her family was her greatest drawback... This was something which went beyond him (Dilip) and he couldn't control the whole situation."

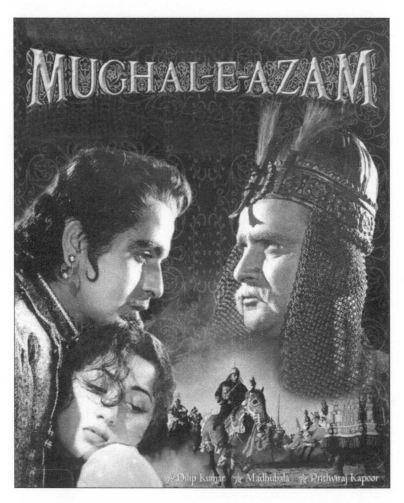

'*Mughal-e-Azam*', released in 1960, became a blockbuster

Dilip Kumar was very bitter and not even on talking terms with Madhubala, except for scenes required for shooting. Under such conditions, Madhubala maintained her serenity and gave her best and super performance in '*Mughal-e-Azam*'. Madhubala, as Anarkali, accepts from Prince Salim, played by her real-life prince, a prize of thorns for winning a singing contest '*Teri mehfil mein kismat azma kar hum bhi dekhenge...*' This concept of emotional involvement was the fact of her love story. While filming '*Mughal-e-Azam*', Director K. Asif was unaware of the extent of Madhubala's physical illness. K. Asif put real chains on her so that she couldn't stand up as the script demanded when she is imprisoned. She was badly cut and her skin turned blue; in some of the scenes she looks pale and sick.

'*Mughal-e-Azam*' was released and became a major blockbuster. Madhubala was nominated for the *Filmfare* Award but lost. Fans suspected that *Filmfare* had been rigged for years and that Madhubala lost because she wouldn't pay bribes. She was just twenty-years old, with a natural buoyant ebullience, when she joined the cast of '*Mughal-e-Azam*'. Her attitude was initially casual and she had no clear idea of how to approach her role. Once she understood what was expected of her and what the demands of the role were, Madhubala rose to the challenge.

'*Mughal-e-Azam*' gave her the opportunity of fulfilling herself totally as an actress, for it was a role that all actresses dream of playing. A number of Anarkalis had already been seen on the screen; the character was not new to the public. It was a challenge to play this well-known, well-loved character and make it successful once again. All doubts were put to rest when Madhubala as Anarkali emerged on the screen, pulsatingly alive, vibrant and three-dimensional.

However, by late 1950s, her health was deteriorating fast and director K. Asif, probably unaware of the extent of her illness, required long shooting schedules that made physical demands on her, whether it was posing as a veiled statue in suffocating make-up for hours under the studio lights or being shackled with heavy chains. It was also a time when Madhubala's relationship with Dilip Kumar was fading out – "The lives of Madhubala and her screen character are consistently seen as overlapping, it is because of the overwhelming sense of loss and tragedy and the unrelenting diktat of destiny that clung to both and which neither could escape."

'*Mughal-e-Azam*' was released on 5 August 1960 and became the biggest grossing film at that time, a record that went unbroken for fifteen years until the release of the film 'Sholay' in 1975. It still ranks second in the list of all-time box-office hits of Indian cinema. Shahida says, "While shooting for 'Mughal-e-Azam', she was tied with chains and had to walk around with them. That was stressful. By the end of the day, her hands would turn blue. She'd even refuse food saying that she had to look anguished and weary for the jail scenes. The 'feather scene' between her and *Bhaijan* (considered the most romantic in Hindi cinema) was shot after the break-up."

Said her co-star in the film, Ajit, "In a scene, where she is running away from the angry Akbar, the shot required her to run quite a distance. As the cameras followed her, capturing every heart-breaking moment, she made the hundred-metre dash. When she collapsed on the floor at the end of the shot, there were tears in every eye." Worst of all was the wearing of iron chains, as displayed in the scene where she sits with her upraised hands, the chains bearing her down. She had to drag them back and forth repeatedly for the rehearsals. Abrasions from the weight of the chains were so severe that she was confined to bed for many days.

Her last released film '*Jwala*', although filmed in the late 1950s, was not released until 1971.

Dilip Kumar clarifies in his autobiography what corroborator what Shahida has to say, "Contrary to popular notions, her father, Ataullah Khan, was not opposed to her marrying me. He had his own production company and he was only too glad to have two stars under the same roof. Had I not seen the whole business from my own point of view, it would have been just what he wanted, that is, Dilip Kumar and Madhubala holding hands and singing duets in his productions till the end of our careers."

Her Married Life

The Dilip Kumar-Madhubala affair had all the ingredients of making a classic love story, but when all her dreams of marrying Dilip Kumar came to a naught, she married Kishore Kumar on the rebound, while a few years later, Dilip Kumar married the 'beauty queen' Saira Banu. Shahida says, "I remember when *Bhaijan* married Saira Banu, *Aapa* was sad because she loved him. She'd say, '*Unke naseeb mein woh* (Saira Banu) *thi, main nahin*'. But she'd also say, 'He's got married to a very pretty girl. She's so devoted. I'm very happy for him.' But a vacuum remained in her heart."

Madhubala was never accepted into Kishore Kumar's family with open arms. The marriage failed to work and within a few weeks, she moved back home to her father and sisters. Again, there are varied reasons as to why the actress returned to her father's house within weeks of signing on the dotted line. Some reveal that she confided to them about how unbearable she found Kishore's miserly habits, but there are others who find this hard to believe. Abrar Alvi speaks in glowing terms of Kishore's large-heartedness. "He never defaulted on payments and always paid generously. He was a very hospitable man and treated me to extravagant spreads, which included Bengali sweets. Madhu went back to her father's house because her weak heart could not take the loud noise of the aeroplanes that flew low over Kishore's house, which was very close to the airport."

Shahida's take on the marriage is, "On the rebound, *Aapa* got involved with Kishore Kumar who was going through a divorce with Ruma Devi Guha Thakurta (actor-singer). What attracted her to Kishore? Maybe it was his singing or maybe his ability to make her laugh. Their love affair went on for three years through '*Chalti ka Naam Gadi*' and '*Half Ticket*'. They got married in 1960, when she was twenty-seven. After marriage they flew to London, where the doctor told her she had only two years to live. After that, Kishore left her at our house saying, 'I can't look after her. I'm on outdoors often.' But she wanted to be with him. He'd visit her once in two months though. Maybe he wanted to detach himself from her so that the final separation wouldn't hurt. But he never abused her as was reported. He bore her medical expenses. They remained married for nine years."

Madhubala and Kishore Kumar in *'Chalti ka Naam Gadi'*

According to Leena Chandavarkar (Kishore Kumar's fourth wife), "When she (Madhubala) realised Dilip was not going to marry her, on the rebound and just to prove to him that she could get whosoever she wanted, she went and married a man she did not even know properly."

B.K. Karanjia surmised, "Madhubala may have felt that perhaps this was her best chance" because by this time she became seriously ill, and was about to stop working completely. "However," he added, "it was a most unlikely union, and not a happy one either."

Madhubala's illness was known to Kishore but like all the others, he did not realise its gravity. Ataullah did not approve of his son-in-law at all but he had lost the will to disapprove. Ashok Kumar, Kishore's brother, told *Filmfare*: "She suffered a lot and her illness made her very bad tempered. She often fought with Kishore and would take off to her father's house where she spent most of her time."

Kishore Kumar had a melodious voice despite not being trained and he could play comical roles with élan. Probably this attracted Madhubala to him, but he did not make a good husband to an ailing wife. Though he married four times and his last wife Leena Chanda-varkar was all praise for him (Madhubala happened to be his second wife), he could not provide support, neither mental nor physical, to Madhubala as his absence from her side made her fear that his attention was caught elsewhere. There were all kinds of rumours afloat that he used to abuse her which forced her to visit music director Naushad's house as she thought that a *faqir* visiting his house would provide her relief from her condition. Naushad had seen her break into tears a number of times and had even advised her to start life afresh by leaving Kishore Kumar. But she used to quote poet Moin Ehsan Jazbi:

Jab kashti saabit-o-saalim thi,

Sahil ki tamanna kisko thi?

Ab aisi shikasta kashti mein

Sahil ki tamanna kaun kare?

(When my boat was sturdy and safe

Who ever thought of the shore?

Now with such a dilapidated boat,

How can I hope to reach ashore?)

Dilip was once asked about Anarkali and told that it was no secret that he had a tempestuous affair with Madhubala, the film's heroine. He did not deny the relationship. So were they really in love when 'Mughal-e-Azam' was made or was it all just acting?

Dilip Kumar was a little evasive. "Frankly," he said finally, "I don't remember the exact timing. Was I carrying on an affair with her when the film was made? Was it before? I don't remember." A breakthrough? He is notoriously reluctant to talk about any of the women in his life, so even this slightly evasive answer about Madhubala marked a break from the past. "Why didn't you marry her?" I persisted. "She was very beautiful. She was a very nice girl," he responded. "She made a conscious attempt to improve herself. By the end, she had even learnt to speak good English." Was her family the problem? He switched over to talk about something else. Saira Banu came to my rescue. "Her father Ataullah Khan was also a Pathan, wasn't he?" she began. She knew her husband well. The response was immediate. "Pathan, my foot! He couldn't speak one word of Pathani! He was no Pathan. He was from Delhi or somewhere." So the family was the problem? But Saira would not let him off so easily, "Is it true that Ataullah Khan wanted you to act in his home production and you refused and this led to a rift?" "How can a man like that expect to make movies?" asked Dilip Kumar, now slightly agitated. "He thought that because of his daughter, I was signed, sealed and delivered." I looked accusingly at Saira. "He's told you the Madhubala story before?" I asked. "No, no," she said. "He never talks about her."

Her Last Days

Shahida recalled that Madhubala as a baby was born 'blue' – a serious sign of cyanosis and poor oxygen perfusion. Madhubala had a ventricualar septal defect (VSD), a disorder colloquially referred to as a hole in the heart. A congenital abnormality of that kind allowed for mixing of both normal oxygenated blood and deoxygenated blood to flow through her body – an unhealthy adulteration with a bad prognosis. While a somewhat common birth defect (one in 500 babies are born with a VSD), the medical community's understanding of the condition was in its infancy. VSD had first been described

in 1879 and at the time of Madhubala's birth, there was
no treatment. Yet Madhubala continued to grow into a
vivacious and beautiful young woman whose fragile
health was for many years known only to a few.

It was not until filming scenes for 'Bahut Din Huwe'
in 1954 when Madhubala vomited blood on the set, that
some came to know of her health. It was an ominous sign
that electrified the Indian media. The history of her heart
defect came to public light as the mid-1950s brought her a
string of failures, earning her the label 'box-office poison'.
With skyrocketing notoriety, no longer was Madhubala's
illness a family secret.

During the filming of the famous song, "Bekas pe
karam kijiye...," Madhubala's performance turned art
into life. The scene was of a defiant courtesan Anarkali
chained in the palace prison, singing for mercy. Director
K. Asif actually made Madhubala perform in heavy,
burdensome metal chains that weighed the actress down
and cut into her skin. Her exhaustion and despair were
real – for a patient with VSD, such an amount of physical
exertion truly mimicked the torture of her character.

By 1960, her condition aggravated. Shahida, speaking
about Kishore Kumar, said, "Yes, she was already sick.

We had decided on going to London for the diagnosis. But Kishore *bhaiya* was adamant. He said, 'Look, she is not sick; nothing's happened to her'. And indeed, she didn't look very sick. My father and others tried to convince Kishore *bhaiya*, 'Let the diagnosis be done in London first, and then you can get married'. But he didn't relent. Finally, the marriage happened and thereafter, they went to London. On coming back from there, I don't know what happened to Kishore *bhaiya*. He came and insisted on her being kept at our house. He said, 'She is very sick, I can't take care of her. Even the doctor has given her a little more time'. We said, 'Whatever little time she has now, she would love to spend with you'. But then he said, 'No, I have to go to shootings'. We suggested he keep a nurse. But again, he didn't relent. So we sisters, till today, have a regret somewhere deep within us, that the love she always desired, she never got."

In 1966, with a slight improvement in her health, she made a valiant attempt to complete her work in '*Chalak*' opposite Raj Kapoor as it needed only a short spell of shooting, but she could not survive the strain of lights and the heat of the studios. The film had perforce to be left incomplete.

Little did her family know that the very same year, on
the other side of the world at the University of Minnesota,
Dr. Walt Lillehei was about to make medical history. After
years of research in the field, on the morning of March
26, 1954, Lillehei performed the first surgical closure on
a child with VSD. The surgery was a success. It brought
hope to thousands of families whose children were other-
wise not expected to live past their 30th birthday. It
became clear that her only hope lay in the rumours of a
surgical cure with the techniques recently pioneered by
Dr. Lillehei. Perhaps if Madhubala had been born just
a few years later or if Dr. Lillehei had begun his famous
experiments just a few years earlier, Madhubala would
have lived to see a surgery that would have allowed her to
celebrate her 80th birthday today with us. Perhaps it was
Madhubala's early death itself that has immortalised her
as a forever beautiful, forever carefree young woman who
will remain always elusive.

It was with a heavy spirit that Madhubala had returned
home to Bombay where she realised her career as an
actress was over. When Sushila Rani, wife of Baburao
Patel went to see her, Madhubala hugged her tight and
sent a message for Baburao, "Tell uncle, it is never too
late to visit the sick." Whenever Sushila Rani recalled

the incident, tears sprang to her eyes, even though decades had passed since then. Shakti Samanta, too, would get visibly moved when he recalled how he got a phone call from her saying, "'I want to meet you. Please come!' When I went over, I found her very thin and unwell but with full make-up on. I asked her, 'Madhu, why are you wearing make-up?' She replied, 'Shakti, you have seen me in my best form. I could not let you see me as I am today'. I found it difficult to check my tears. Such a fabulous person, such a great artiste and she was talking like this! She was very depressed."

Her sisters never stop acknowledging what all she did for her. Shahida says, "My sister was like a godmother to us. We owe our life to her. But even though she worked so hard, she never got to see the world or enjoy it. For her, it was just work, home; work, home."

Shahida adds, "The hole in her heart was detected when she was shooting for S.S. Vasan's 'Chalak' in Madras 1954. She had vomited blood. She was advised bed-rest for three months but continued working as she did not want her film to suffer. Due to her ailment, her body would produce extra blood. So it would spill out from the nose and mouth. The doctor would come home and extract bottles of blood. She also suffered from pulmonary pressure of the lungs. She coughed all the time. Every four to five hours she had to be given oxygen or else would get breathless. She was confined to bed for nine years and was reduced to just bones and skin. She'd keep crying, '*Mujhe zinda rehna hai, mujhe marna nahin hai. Doctor kab ilaaj nikalenge* (I want to live. I don't want to die. Wonder when the doctors will find a cure!).'

"If a twenty-seven-year-old is told that she has two years to live, what would her state be?" asks sister Shahida. Any wonder then that through her last years, *"Rulake gaya sapna mera…"* (from *'Jewel Thief'*) was the song Madhubala kept listening to!

Ironically, after her Valentine's Day birthday, Madhubala died at the young age of thirty-six, on February 23, 1969 from a hole in her heart. Says Shahida, "During her (Madhubala's) last days, I was suffering from chicken-pox and so was advised to keep away from her. But when the doctor said that she was sinking, I rushed up to see her. But she had passed away. She was only thirty-six to my nineteen. Though *Bhaijan* never visited her when she was unwell, he flew down from Madras to pay his last respects at the *qabristan* (cemetery). Food was sent from his home to ours for three days (as is the custom)."

As Dilip Kumar was shooting at Madras for the film '*Gopi*', he could not bid her goodbye but visited the cemetery to do so before offering his condolences to the family. Shammi Kapoor said, "Both Shakti Samanta and I had loved her and we both cried when we heard the news."

Friend and film star Nadira said, "The day she passed away, I was at the race course. I remember I sat down and asked myself, 'Will I be able to go there and see that beautiful face with its eyes closed?' I couldn't bear the thought of seeing her dead. There are some people you want to remember in all their vivaciousness – smiling, giggling. You just don't want to see them dead. They live forever and ever. She was one of them."

Filmfare wrote: "In the dimmed starlight, she was a bird whose wings had been clipped, a child robbed of its enchantment. Lonely and alone…"

Her erstwhile beau Premnath wrote a poem in farewell:

"Laid to rest my love

My darling,

My would-have-been wife,

I saw you to the end of your grave…

Wish you had spoken to me your farewell

Mighty Venus of the Indian screen

Now matted to Earth."

Some say her death was due to a broken heart; others say it was from the congenital heart disease, but no one will ever know the truth. The bubbly actress was cheated of her dreams and lived only for thirty-six years to become a star forever…

She was buried with her personal diary at the Santa Cruz Muslim cemetery by her father Ataullah and husband Kishore Kumar. She had expressed her desire to see Dilip Kumar the day before she breathed her last. People say that Dilip Kumar regularly placed flowers over her tomb, which was built with marble and carried inscriptions of *aayats* from the *Quran* along with verse dedications. This too was put an end to when her tomb was demolished in 2010 to make space for new graves. Shahida says, "A few years back her tomb was demolished as it was in a Wahabi (a Muslim sect that doesn't allow building of tombs) cemetery. They wiped away the last memories of a legend." It is said Ataullah Khan was a broken man who could not recover from the trauma of her death and during the remaining years of his life he regretted his failure to place his daughter's favourite bottle of perfume in her grave.

With Kishore Kumar, the scenario was bizarre. With feelings for each other just as strong, with no other individuals creeping into either of their lives, they persisted in proceeding to destroy their relationship almost as if compelled by forces beyond them. In the space of about five to six years, by choosing to become Mrs. Kishore Kumar, Madhubala took the most irrational decision of her life. The general reaction to her marriage to Kishore Kumar was echoed in Nadira's incredulous disbelief: "From the sublime to the ridiculous! Oh my God! Madhu what are you doing?"

Madhubala's strong presence in public memory is seen when one reads all recent polls about top actresses or beauties of the Indian cinema and her name is on top. Every year, on her birthday, numerous articles are printed and TV programmes aired to commemorate her. Her posters are still in demand and sold alongside contemporary actresses, and modern magazines continue to publish stories on her personal life and career, often

promoting her name heavily on the covers to attract sales.
Many believe, however, Madhubala remains one of the
most underrated actresses as "her beauty attracted more
attention than her talent."

Dilip Kumar admits that he did try to sort out his
differences with Ataullah Khan regarding entering
into a professional contract while agreeing to marry
her but, "my instructs, however, predicted a situation
in which I would be trapped and all the hard work
and dedication I had invested in my career would be
blown away by a helpless surrender to someone else's
dictates and strategies...The scenario was not very
pleasant and it was heading inevitably to a dead end.
In the circumstances, therefore, it seemed best that
we did not decide to marry..."

Interesting Facts

First Love Affair

Kamal Amrohi directed Madhubala for his film
'*Mahal*' and it is said he used to spend hours fussing
around over her *dupatta* so as to give her a covered,
virginal image, his favourite, even as she looked on
lovingly, occasionally giggling at his laborious attention
to little things which really did not matter much to her.
This was perhaps the happiest period of her life. Her love
affair with Amrohi continued even after '*Mahal*' was
released in 1949. Father Ataullah Khan was aware of this
affair, but as he was in awe of Kamal Amrohi, he used

to say, "*Aage chalke in dono ki shaadi ho jaaye to mujhe koyi aitraaz nahin hai*" (I have no objection if both will get married in the near future). But Madhubala did not want to share him with Amrohi's first wife and insisted on him taking divorce from his first wife so that she could marry him. Amrohi was not willing to do this and used to tell her, "*Baatne se pyar badhta hai*" (When you share your love, it increases). She even went to the extent of offering him lakhs of rupees provided he left his first wife. Amrohi remained loyal to his first wife and told Madhubala that he could not sell his wife and children and nor his conscience! So Madhubala broke off with him, never to see him again. However, this story is rejected by Madhubala's sister who calls it a figment of imagination.

'Jwar Bhata'

Madhubala, who was to appear in '*Jwar Bhata*', in which Dilip Kumar was playing the lead role, was unable to work in the film, but this was the moment the youngster first set eyes on Dilip Kumar. They met each other seven years later on the sets of '*Tarana*' when she was eighteen-years old. During the shooting, she sent her hairdresser with a note written in Urdu and a red rose, asking him to accept it if he loved her. This intrigued and amused him but naturally he accepted the rose.

Dilip Kumar, who could set many a girl's heart aflutter with his slow smile and the quiet intensity of his eyes, was not the frivolous, flippant kind; he was drawn, on his part, to his lively and vivacious co-star of *'Tarana'* and it was the depth and seriousness of his feelings for her that made Premnath decide to step aside willingly and relinquish his own suit.

'Tarana'

The early '50s were Madhubala's best years. She was rapturously and ecstatically in love and exuded happiness. Recalling those days, Gulshan Ewing says, "She thrust on me the mantle of 'confidante'. Many were the whispered conversations she had with me, all rustling with the same rhythm – 'Yusuf, Yusuf, Yusuf'. She was so in love, the light leapt out and dazzled everyone. She would squeal when his name was mentioned; she would blush and perspire when his presence was imminent."

'Mr. & Mrs. 55'

This incident talks of the time when, in her personal life, her love affair with Dilip Kumar was at its peak. She was shooting for Guru Dutt's '*Mr. & Mrs. 55*' at Mehboob Studio. Abrar Alvi, the film's scriptwriter, narrates the incident thus: "The scene to be shot had Lalita Pawar showing Madhubala a photograph of her husband in a compromising position with another woman. It was a ruse to make the heroine file for divorce. Since we didn't have the relevant photograph at the time of the shoot, we borrowed a photograph of the same size, from Mehboob Khan's office, with the intention of inserting the right one later on. Now, it so happened that the one we borrowed was a photograph of Dilip Kumar. When Madhu saw it, she just refused to do the scene. 'I can't concentrate,' she pleaded. 'Please get another photograph.' No amount of cajoling helped. Ultimately, we had to do as she wished."

Father Ataullah Khan

Madhubala's father was a stern and dominating person and Madhubala was in awe of him all her life. When it came to the crunch, despite the depth of her feelings for Dilip Kumar, she did not have the courage to defy and over-ride her father and marry without his approval. Her happiness hinged on both Dilip Kumar's love and her father's acceptance of it. Her father was rendered unquestioning obedience, love and respect. In fact, it is said that when Dilip Kumar started his own production 'Ganga Jamuna', he even decided to give the entire profits of the film to Ataullah Khan so that he and Madhubala could get married and she could stop working.

"I cannot think of marriage," she would say, "till I have fulfilled my responsibilities to my family". And yet, by the mid-fifties, there were clear indications that she was nearing a decision. In 1955, she made a bold declaration in a *Filmfare* interview: "Nobody in the world has any right to interfere with one's choice of a husband. I would marry only the man with whom I am very much in love."

Without distraction, Madhubala had faced Dilip Kumar in 'Mughal-e-Azam', which took ten years to make. By now Ataullah Khan, as a domineering father, did his best to keep Dilip away from Madhubala. However, like Romeo and Juliet, Dilip and Madhubala found ways to see each other; sometimes at a common friend's home and if not, there were always the film sets. They found ways and means of meeting each other, away from Ataullah Khan's disapproving eye – sometimes in Sushila Rani's house, sometimes in her make-up room.

'Naya Daur'

Dilip and Madhubala had both been signed and were
well into pre-production for the B.R. Chopra's film '*Naya
Daur*'. In the film, a forty-day shooting schedule had been
allotted to take place on location in Bhopal. Ataullah
Khan refused to let Madhubala do the location shoot,
claiming the scenes could be shot in a studio. B.R. Chopra
told Khan that the 40-day location shoot was essential.
Now it was well known that Ataullah Khan had always
refused to let Madhubala do location shoots, citing the
reason as her fragile health. Dilip Kumar was certain that
Ataullah would not let her go because the pair would be
unchaperoned on a location shoot for forty days. Madhubala herself was caught in the middle; finally she opted to
follow whatever decision her father demanded. Eventually, Madhubala was dropped from the film and replaced
by Vyjayantimala.

Ataullah sued B.R. Chopra, who counter sued.
Eventually the whole fiasco was dragged into court. At
some point in the trial, the personal relationship between
Dilip Kumar and Madhubala was put down as evidence,
and their whole affair came under the spotlight. The
press had a field day and the public relished every word

of the published court transcripts. Dilip, feeling very bitter, had of course sided with B.R. Chopra and presented evidence against Ataullah Khan and Madhubala. Dilip Kumar appeared as a witness for the prosecution against Madhubala and said some very bitter things about her in open court. While Dilip was testifying against her, she turned to her lawyer R.D. Chadha and said, "I don't believe this is the man who was so in love with me and whom I loved more than anyone and anything in the world." The elder Khan presented evidence against Chopra and Kumar. It spelled disaster for the couple. At one point in the trial, a distraught Dilip Kumar, under cross-examination on the witness stand, declared, "I love this woman and shall love her till my dying day." Dilip Kumar allowed himself a rare moment of public vulnerability: "I love Madhubala and shall always love her," he said. Madhubala gulped down her tears.

Dilip Kumar never came back to her and the 'Naya Daur' court case and its fallout sounded the death knell for her, ending any chance of redeeming the relationship. Too much was said and done that could not be forgotten. Madhubala, who was shocked and angry in the aftermath of the case, made an attempt at reconciliation, but Dilip Kumar evidently did not forgive her.

But it seems the pair continued to long for each other, much after their tragic break-up.

Estrangement

The well-known journalist and writer, Bunny Reuben, speaks of her unsuccessful effort to reach out to the estranged Dilip. Assigned to do a feature on her for *Filmfare*, Reuben was surprised to be given an appointment at her home and not at the studios as usual. He was further taken aback when he was escorted straight to her room upstairs. She seemed very keen to meet him and it struck him that the reason was his well-known proximity to Dilip Kumar that had prompted her to send for him in preference to her friend, Gulshan Ewing.

The article was outlined to her but in the meeting, which stretched for over two hours, she spoke instead on the subject closest to her heart. "She wanted to talk only about her Yusuf Khan; doing the feature was secondary. As she proceeded to unburden herself of all the intimate and hurtful details of their relationship, she put her head on my shoulders and wept uncontrollably," recollects Reuben.

Reuben understood that she was trying to send a message across to Dilip. "She wanted me to go and convince him how badly he had treated her and how much she still loved him." Moved by her tears, Reuben looked for a suitable opportunity to report the whole episode to Dilip Kumar, but found that Dilip was in no mood to listen.

He had hardly gone beyond the opening sentence: "She still carries a torch for you, Yusuf," when he was cut short and curtly dismissed by an angry retort, "What bloody torch?" Not even the essentials of his two-hour conversation with the unhappy Madhubala could be conveyed. In keeping with the spirit of the age, and *Filmfare's* policy in particular, the star's troubled outpourings were not betrayed in print. There was no 'scoop'.

Meanwhile, '*Mughal-e-Azam*' was still on the floors. Its shooting constantly brought Dilip and Madhubala together, but could not heal the scars. Unable to work out a rapprochement, she channelised her distress and pent-up grief into her characterisation of the unfortunate Anarkali. The role assumed sublime proportions.

A change began to come over Madhubala, impercep-
tible at first but quite apparent to those who knew her.
A friend described it thus: "In 1951, when I first knew
her, she was always smiling. I envied her peace of mind.
By 1958, the beauty was still there but the peace of mind
had vanished."

The same year, *Filmfare* observed: "Her laughter is a
becoming quality, not only because she comes to life as
it were when she laughs but because a smile is the most
charming cloak for a sob…Madhubala has had her share
of struggle, suffering, disillusionment and emotional
shock but no matter what lies beneath the surface, she
cloaks it with a graceful smile."

Madhubala Drowns Herself in Work

For the next few years, she followed the time-honoured
antidote for heart-break and, turning to her work, tried to
forget her troubles. She had the satisfaction of working in a
number of highly successful films, like '*Kala Pani*', '*Howrah
Bridge*', '*Chalti ka Naam Gaadi*' and '*Barsaat ki Raat*'.
On the personal front, she made an admirable bid to
maintain a facade of normalcy, but a wistfulness and a
lost look began to lurk under the surface. The fabulous
smile no longer reached her eyes. "She must have been

miserable, but she wouldn't show it," commented Sushila Rani Patel, while Gulshan Ewing observed, "An ethereal beauty, whose eyes were always sad, but whose lips were always smiling." But in the presence of long-time

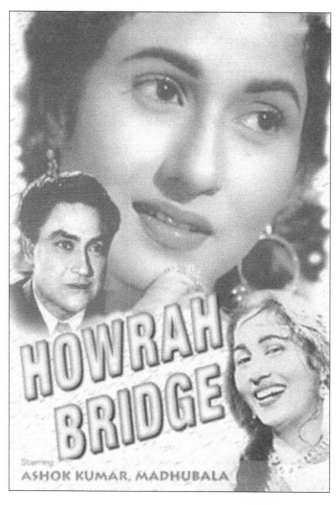

Madhubala and Ashok Kumar in *'Howrah Bridge'*

colleagues or in the privacy of her make-up room, there were times when sobs racked Madhubala. It seemed the pair continued to pine for each other, far after their break-up. Dilip Kumar, a disillusioned man, turned to alcohol and eventually married Saira Banu. Bharat Bhushan, Pradeep Kumar and Kishore Kumar proposed to her but she chose to marry the last named of the three. It is said that she and Kishore Kumar argued and bickered constantly. Plunged into a loveless marriage with him, Madhubala soon realised she had made a mistake in marrying him, as she truly loved and desperately wanted to marry Dilip.

Views of Madhubala's Sister

In an interview, Madhubala's sister claimed that Madhubala loved Dilip Kumar till her last day, but clarified that her father was not to blame for their break-up. "What a lot of rubbish, but it puts an end to the rumours that Madhubala had many affairs. She loved Dilip Saheb till the day she died," she added. "The reason Madhubala broke up with Dilip Kumar was B.R. Chopra's film 'Naya Daur', not my father. Madhubala had shot a part of the film when the makers decided to go for an outdoor shoot to Gwalior. The place was known for dacoits, so my father asked them to change the location. They disagreed because they wanted a hilly terrain. So my father asked her to quit the film.

"Chopra's production house filed a case against her, which went on for a year. But this did not spoil their relationship. Dilip Saheb told her to forget movies and get married to him. She said she would marry him, provided he apologise to her father. He refused, so Madhubala left him. That one 'sorry' could have changed her life. She loved Dilip Saheb till the last day," she concluded.

Nadira's Comments

The perceptive Nadira saw it too: "She considered herself married to him. They were almost married. She wore his ring, he wore hers." Dilip Kumar himself acknowledged it in a statement to a newspaper, saying that the proposal had been sent by him. A film journalist of the time, Ram Aurangabadkar reported that Dilip Kumar sent his eldest sister, *Badi Aapa*, to Madhubala's house with the marriage proposal, saying they'd like it to be in seven days. Ataullah Khan turned it down.

The Break-up

Lower and lower did her spirits sink, for, many believed she was still in love with Dilip Kumar and lower and lower did her health fall. She had kept her sickness a secret for so long. For many years, she had suffered from a hole in her heart, but only her family knew. Many times, she collapsed on the sets and they thought that she was delicate. Madhubala allowed them to believe that, for, in '*Mughal-e-Azam*', you can see her pain with the real chains on her and beads of sweat on her face in the scene where she and Nigar Sultana sing a debate on love, "*Muhabbat hum ne maana ke zindagi barbaad karti hai, yeh kya kum hai ki mar jaaney pe duniya yaad karti hai…*" (We may be doomed in our love life, but is it not something that after our departure from Earth, the world misses us?)

'*Mughal-e-Azam*' Revisited

During the Mughal era, the *shahi paigham* or the 'royal message' was sent with pomp to deliver a message from the Emperor himself. Over four decades after the release of the historic '*Mughal-e-Azam*', the one and only Prince Salim, i.e. Dilip Saheb was once again presented with a *farmaan*. This time the occasion was the release of the colour '*Mughal-e-Azam*' DVD and VCD by Shemaroo Video. In an innovative presentation, Shemaroo's 'Royal Messenger' visited Dilip Kumar at his residence, read out a *farmaan* in Urdu to announce the release of the '*Mughal-*

e-Azam' DVD and take the honour of presenting a copy to Dilip Saheb. For a movie that has been so widely written and appreciated, Shemaroo Video decided to come out with an innovative and novel approach in its presentation.

Apparently happy on receiving the colour DVD of *'Mughal-e-Azam'*, Dilip Kumar and Saira Banu relived the nostalgia of the movie's black-and-white and colour premieres and how times had changed since then.

At the release of the DVD, Dilip Kumar expressed his happiness at the print. What is more, Madhubala's poster was put up at his house. Dilip Kumar admitted that he still remembered all the dialogues of the film and could recite them without having to read them again. His wife Saira Banu said that it was after a long gap of forty years that Dilip Kumar had visited the Eros Theatre to watch any film.

On being asked if it was Dilip Kumar's idea to restore and colour the print of *'Mughal-e-Azam'*, Dilip Kumar replied, "Yes, I had made the suggestion to the son of the late Shapoorji Pallonji. The idea had been discussed with the Indian Academy of Arts & Animation, that does a lot of work for foreign countries and specialises in the art of fine paintings. Sterling Investment Corporation Pvt. Ltd. approved the proposal and the project got underway."

Dilip Kumar was told that the industry lore had it that when Asif Saheb approached Ustad Bade Ghulam Ali Khan to sing Tansen's, '*Prem jogan ban jaoon…*', the maestro was not too keen. He insisted on seeing the scene first. So it was hurriedly edited and shown to him. It was a moonlit night and Prince Salim was in the palace garden, cradling Anarkali's head and caressing her cheek with a feather. Ustadji was so struck by the beautiful Anarkali and her handsome prince that he sang the song four times and each time, the reel had to be rewound and screened for him.

Dilip Kumar replied, "Yes, Ustad Bade Ghulam Ali Khan Saheb insisted on seeing the film first, but I don't think he agreed to sing the song because of the beautiful Anarkali. No doubt Madhubala was a beautiful lady, but I think he was finally convinced by what he saw; by what we had shot."

Dilip Saheb was so emotional at the end of the '*Mughal-e-Azam*' re-release premiere that at the end of the film, his eyes filled with tears. He said, "To dig back memories, it involves effort. Memories so often go to sleep within the mind. Sometimes it becomes painful when you think of a tragic incident." He ended on a touching note, "I wish Allah were to bring back the people in the film who are no longer here with us."

Filmography

Year	Film	Director	Notes
1942	Basant	Amiya Chakravorty	as Manju
1944	Mumtaz Mahal	Kidar Sharma	as a child artiste
1945	Dhanna Bhagat	Kidar Sharma	as a child artiste
1946	Pujari	Aspi Irani	as a child artiste
1946	Phoolwari	Chaturbhuj Doshi	as a child artiste
1946	Rajputani	Aspi Irani	as a child artiste
1947	Neel Kamal	Kidar Sharma	First film as a heroine
1947	Chittor Vijay	Mohan Sinha	
1947	Mere Bhagwan	Mohan Sinha	

Year	Film	Director	Notes
1947	Khoobsurat Duniya	Mohan Sinha	
1947	Dil ki Rani	Mohan Sinha	as Raj Kumari Singh
1948	Parai Aag	Najm Naqvi	
1948	Lal Dupatta	K.B. Lall	
1948	Desh Sewa	N. Vakil	
1948	Amar Prem	N.M. Kelkar	
1949	Sipahiya	Aspi Irani	
1949	Singaar	J.K. Nanda	
1949	Paras	Anant Thakur	as Priya
1949	Neki aur Badi	Kidar Sharma	
1949	Mahal	Kamal Amrohi	as Kamini
1949	Imtihaan	Mohan Sinha	
1949	Dulari	A.R. Kardar	as Shobha/Dulari
1949	Daulat	Sohrab Modi	
1949	Apradhi	Y. Pethkar	as Sheela Rani
1950	Pardes	M. Sadiq	as Chanda
1950	Nishana	Wajahat Mirza	as Greta
1950	Nirala	Devendra Mukherjee	as Poonam
1950	Madhubala	Prahlad Dutt	
1950	Hanste Aansu	K.B. Lall	
1950	Beqasoor	K. Amarnath	as Usha
1951	Tarana	Ram Daryani	as Tarana
1951	Saiyan	M. Sadiq	as Saiyan

Year	Film	Director	Notes
1951	Nazneen	N.K. Ziree	
1951	Nadaan	Hira Singh	
1951	Khazana	M. Sadiq	
1951	Badal	Amiya Chakravorty	as Ratna
1951	Aaram	D.D. Kashyap	as Leela
1952	Saqi	H.S. Rawail	as Rukhsana
1952	Deshabakthan	Amiya Chakravorty	
1952	Sangdil	R.C. Talwar	
1953	Rail ka Dibba	P.N. Arora	as Chanda
1953	Armaan	Fali Mistri	
1954	Bahut Din Huye	S.S. Vasan	as Chandrakanta
1954	Amar	Mehboob Khan	as Anju
1955	Teerandaz	H.S. Rawail	
1955	Naqab	Lekhraj Bhakri	
1955	Naata	D.N. Madhok	as Tara
1955	Mr. & Mrs. '55	Guru Dutt	as Anita Verma
1956	Shirin Farhad	Aspi Irani	as Shirin
1956	Raj Hath	Sohrab Modi	as Raja Beti/Rajkumari
1956	Dhake ki Malmal	J.K. Nanda	
1957	Yahudi ki Ladki	S.D. Narang	
1957	Gateway of India	Om Prakash	as Anju

Year	Film	Director	Notes
1957	Ek Saal	Devendra Goel	as Usha Sinha
1958	Police	Kali Das	
1958	Phagun	Bibhuti Mitra	as Banani
1958	Kala Pani	Raj Khosla	as Asha
1958	Howrah Bridge	Shakti Samanta	as Edna
1958	Chalti ka Naam Gaadi	Satyen Bose	as Renu
1958	Baghi Sipahi	Bhagwandas Varma	
1959	Kal Hamara Hai	S.K. Prabhakar	as Madhu/Bela
1959	Insaan Jaag Utha	Shakti Samanta	as Gauri
1959	Do Ustad (1959)	Tara Harish	as Madhu Sharma
1960	Mehlon ke Khwab	Hyder	as Asha
1960	Jaali Note	Shakti Samanta	as Renu/Beena
1960	Barsaat Ki Raat	P.L. Santoshi	as Shabnam
1960	Mughal-e-Azam	K. Asif	as Anarkali; Nominated—Filmfare Award for Best Actress
1961	Passport	Pramod Chakraborty	as Rita Bhagwandas
1961	Jhumroo	Shankar Mukherji	as Anjana

Year	Film	Director	Notes
1961	Boy Friend	Naresh Saigal	as Sangeeta
1962	Half Ticket	Kali Das	as Rajnidevi/Asha
1964	Sharabi	Raj Rishi	as Kamala
1971	Jwala	M.V. Raman	

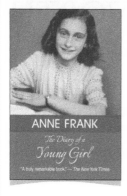

ANNE FRANK

The Diary of a Young Girl
by Anne Frank

Price : Rs. 275
Pages : 224
Size : 7.75x5.25 inches
Binding : Paperback
Language : English
Subject : Memoirs
ISBN : 9789380914312

The Diary of a Young Girl started two days before Anne Frank's thirteenth birthday. In 1942, the Nazis had occupied Holland, and her family left their home to go into hiding, as they were Jews. Anne Frank recorded daily events, her personal experiences and her feelings in her diary for the next two years. Cut off from the outside world, she and her family faced hunger, boredom, claustrophobia at living in confined quarters, and the ever-present threat of discovery and death. One day, she and her family were betrayed and taken away to the Bergen-Belsen concentration camp, where she eventually died.

It is a record of a sensitive girl's tragic experience during one of the worst periods in human history. This diary is so powerful that it leaves a deep impact on the mind of its readers.

"A truly remarkable book."

—The New York Times

KNOW YOUR WORTH

Stop Thinking, Start Doing

by

NK Sondhi & Vibha Malhotra

The secret behind the success of most of the people is not what they do, but how they do it!

This book discusses the life-changing concepts through storytelling. You would find yourself closely connected to these stories. They will encourage you to explore your own potential to inspire you, and to achieve your real worth. This book will also help you to understand the traits that keep you from achieving your dreams. The book lays down a process to help you emerge from the clutches of negativity and develop a positive approach towards life.

By investing time in yourself, acknowledging your potential, setting a worthy goal, avoiding common traps, surviving bad days and harvesting the power of thoughts, you can be successful.

Read this interesting book to Know Your Worth.

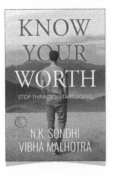

Price : Rs. 295
Pages : 224
Size : 7.75x5.25 inches
Binding : Paperback
Language : English
Subject : Self-Help
ISBN : 9788180320231

OTHER HARDBACK BOOKS

» 1984 by George Orwell
  Fiction/Classics, ISBN: 9788193545836

» Abraham Lincoln by Lord Charnwood
  Biography/Leaders, ISBN: 9789387669147

» Alice's Adventures in Wonderland by Lewis Carroll
  Children's/Classics, ISBN: 9789387669055

» Animal Farm by George Orwell
  Fiction/Classics, ISBN: 9789387669062

» Gitanjali by Rabindranath Tagore
  Fiction/Poetry, ISBN: 9789387669079

» Great Speeches of Abraham Lincoln by Abraham Lincoln
  History/General, ISBN: 9789387669154

» How to Stop Worrying and Start Living by Dale Carnegie
  Self-Help/General, ISBN: 9789387669161

» How to Win Friends and Influence People by Dale Carnegie
  Self-Help/Success, ISBN: 9789387669178

» Illust. Biography of William Shakespeare by Manju Gupta
  Biography/Authors, ISBN: 9789387669246

» Madhubala by Manju Gupta
  Biography/Actors, ISBN: 9789387669253

» Mansarover 1 (Hindi) by Premchand
  Fiction/Short Stories, ISBN: 9789387669086

» Mansarover 2 (Hindi) by Premchand
  Fiction/Short Stories, ISBN: 9789387669093

» Mein Kampf (My Struggle) by Adolf Hitler
  Biography/Leaders, ISBN: 9789387669260

» My Experiments with Truth by Mahatma Gandhi
  Biography/Leaders, ISBN: 9789387669277

» Relativity by Albert Einstein
  Sciences/Physics, ISBN: 9789387669185

OTHER HARDBACK BOOKS

» Selected Stories of Tagore by Rabindranath Tagore
  Fiction/Short Stories, ISBN: 9789387669307

» Sense and Sensibility by Jane Austen
  Fiction/Classics, ISBN: 9789387669109

» Siddhartha by Hermann Hesse
  Fiction/Classics, ISBN: 9789387669116

» Tales from India by Rudyard Kipling
  Fiction/Short Stories, ISBN: 9789387669123

» Tales from Shakespeare by Charles & Mary Lamb
  Children's/Classics, ISBN: 9789387669314

» The Art of War by Sun Tzu
  Self-Help/Success, ISBN: 9789387669321

» The Autobiography of a Yogi by Paramahansa Yogananda
  Biography/General, ISBN: 9789387669192

» The Diary of a Young Girl by Anne Frank
  Biography/General, ISBN: 9789387669208

» The Jungle Book by Rudyard Kipling
  Children's/Classics, ISBN: 9789387669338

» The Light of Asia by Sir Edwin Arnold
  Religion/Buddhism, ISBN: 9789387669130

» The Miracles of Your Mind by Joseph Murphy
  Self-Help/Success, ISBN: 9789387669215

» The Origin of Species by Charles Darwin
  Sciences/Life Sciences, ISBN: 9789387669345

» The Power of Your Subconscious Mind by Joseph Murphy
  Self-Help/General, ISBN: 9789387669222

» The Science of Getting Rich by Wallace D. Wattles
  Self-Help/Success, ISBN: 9789387669239

» Think and Grow Rich by Napoleon Hill
  Self-Help/Success, ISBN: 9789387669352

Lightning Source UK Ltd.
Milton Keynes UK
UKHW012035070519
342287UK00004B/67/P